My Baby
My Grief
My Love

A pregnancy loss journal

Second Edition

JULIE ANN BRYANT

My Baby, My Grief, My Love: A pregnancy loss journal
© Julie Ann Bryant 2024

ISBN: 978-1-923501-40-9

First edition published 2024
Second edition published 2025

Cover Image: Julie Ann Bryant 2018

Cover Design: Busybird Publishing 2025

Layout and Typesetting: Busybird Publishing 2025

Except as provided by the Copyright Act 1968, no part of this publication may be reproduced or communicated to the public without the prior written permission of the publisher.

GENRE: Non-fiction. Bereavement, Grief and Loss. Psychology, Self-help.

Busybird Publishing
2/118 Para Road
Montmorency, Victoria
Australia 3094
www.busybird.com.au

Contents

Foreword by Megan Warren	1
Preface	5
Introduction	11
A Note Regarding The Second Edition Of This Book	17
How To Use This Book	19
Take Good Care Of You	23
Contacts	28
Chapter One: My Baby	31
Your Sweet Baby Forever	32
Where It All Began	34
Your Pregnancy	36
In A Perfect World	38
The Day Everything Changed Forever	40
The First Of Many Goodbyes	42
What Has Helped You Hang On?	44
A Sweet Memory	46
Perfect In Every Way	48
Chapter Two: My Grief	51
The Process Of Grief	52
You Feel Sad, Just So Sad	54
And You Feel So Many Other Things As Well	56

The Questions Grief Asks	58
Those Sleepless Nights	60
Time Stands Still But Life Doesn't Wait	62
Complex Grief, Simple Needs	64
Those "What If" Moments	66
If Your Living Child Is A Surviving Twin	68
Your Partner	70
Who You Are Because Of Your Grief	72
What Was Helpful At The Time Of Your Loss?	74
However, Not Everything Is Helpful	76
Those Tricky Conversations	78
What Would You Like Other Grieving Parents To Know?	80
Chapter Three: My Love	**83**
My Grief, My Love	84
A Special Place For Remembering	86
Give Your Love A Memory	88
Your Baby's Special Day	90
Other Family-Oriented Days	92
Your Own Traditions	94
Love Letter To Your Baby	96
Signs From Heaven	98
Taking That Next Brave Step	100

Chapter Four: Self-Care Plan — 103
    You Are The Expert Of You — 104
    Mental/Emotional Well-being — 106
    Physical Well-being — 110
    Social Needs — 112
    Spiritual Connection — 114
    Poem: Beautiful, Inside and Out — 116

Self-Citations — 119
Acknowledgements — 120
About The Author — 125

This book is dedicated to the memory of our twin daughter Meggie and

_____
I INVITE YOU TO WRITE YOUR BABY'S NAME HERE

whose tiny footprints have left an indelible imprint on our hearts.

Foreword

by Megan Warren

My Baby, My Grief, My Love (2025: 2nd Edn)

I was truly honoured when Julie emailed me and asked me to write the Foreword for this book, which was followed by a case of writers' block.

Julie and I "met" in an online peer support group for mums who have experienced pregnancy loss. (I'll qualify this by saying that despite knowing each other and keeping in touch for over 20 years, we have yet to meet in person.)

It was early 2001, I had recently experienced the loss of my third child – Cianan – and was navigating life following multiple miscarriages, a stillbirth and a neonatal death. Julie was pregnant with Meggie and her twin brother and had just received the news that Meggie had died. We connected in that space and have supported each other from a distance.

Journalling was something I came back to after the loss of our sons, and I now maintain a daily writing practice. It became a haven amid my loss and grief. I have journalled regularly for over 20 years, at times more prolific than others, particularly during the years that I was pregnant and experienced the death of my sons. Those journals now inform my writing and research in creative writing and pregnancy loss.

The grief can be all-consuming with emotions, feelings, questions and memories crowding your thoughts, and you are trying to make sense of the world you find yourself in. I found it useful to get these thoughts out of my head and written down in my journal. That's okay if you have an established practice or experience of journalling.

What happens if you have never journalled, or you don't know where to begin following the loss of your precious baby? Julie has expertly created a series of thoughtful writing prompts to guide you through the process.

My Baby, My Grief, My Love (2025: 2nd Edn)

What I love about this resource that Julie has created, is that it begins with your baby and the significance of their name. So often when we have lost a baby, people don't use their names – they become "the baby". Thank you, Julie, for putting our babies front and centre in the telling of their stories, before we focus on any other detail.

To you, the grieving parent reading this, I am sorry for the loss of your baby. I hope that this book is a safe place for you to tell the story of your precious baby.

Megan Warren
Writer & PhD candidate

Preface

My Baby, My Grief, My Love (2025: 2nd Edn)

There is something very cathartic about seeing your words, your thoughts, in black-and-white in front of you. This is especially true for when you are seeking to understand and make sense of a traumatic event in your life. I began writing poetry as a teenager. In my 20s, 30s, 40s and beyond, my writing has continued in the form of journalling as I have sought to make sense of some traumatic experiences I had faced as a young woman.

The process of trying to conceive isn't always as straightforward as it seems. It becomes even more complicated when an infertility diagnosis is made. My infertility journey began in the mid-80s, spanning some 15 years and once I was under the care of my reproductive gynaecologist, we had 10 stimmed cycles. The accumulated disappointment of each failed cycle was so crushing that I faced the possibility of remaining childless. We took a year-long break from my fertility treatments and went overseas. It was on the aeroplane, homeward-bound to Sydney, that I said to my husband "Let's give it one more try".

It goes without saying that the most traumatic, the most profound loss I have ever experienced was that of my babies. We conceived five babies through our first IVF (in 2000). On day five, following our IVF procedure, three of our blastocysts succumbed and we had a twin-embryo transfer. Sadly, at the mid-pregnancy ultrasound we learned that our precious twin 2, who we named Meggie, had died and I went on to carry both babies to full-term.

With our second IVF (in 2003) we had a total of 18 blastocysts that cycle, with 5 of them succumbing and on day five we had another twin-embryo transfer. Our remaining 11 embryos were put on ice. A few years later,

(c) Julie Ann Bryant

when we knew our family was complete, our frozen embryos were donated to IVF research with the knowledge that they would ultimately help other couples also trying to conceive.

I am ever so grateful for the expertise of the reproductive gynaecologist who helped our dream of parenthood become a reality. Infertility is not a journey I would have chosen for myself, however, the experiences and knowledge I have acquired along the way have helped shape me into the person I am today.

Our two living children are now adults and we are so thankful to have them in our arms. We are beyond proud of who they have grown up to be.

The loss of a blastocyst – the fertilised egg in it's pre-embryonic state – is quite devastating when a couple is going through IVF. So much emotion and hope is invested in the process of trying to conceive. They may just be eggs, however, for a couple dearly wanting to start their family – to welcome a child into their lives – those eggs are their hope for the future. You only have to look in the mirror to see the potential held in each of those little babies lost along the way.

Each loss is a different kind of loss. When you are processing the grief each time, it is still quite profound. Each loss, regardless of the gestational age it occurred, deserves to be grieved.

Experiencing a profound loss leaves you needing a safe haven, a soft place to fall and simply be with your grief. In so many ways, my journals have been my safe haven, my soft place – where many a time, I have fallen and simply been with my grief. My journals have been my constant companion as I worked through my experiences of grief on a very private level.

As a child on the autism spectrum, I had a rich inner world and quite happily existed within it (it should come as no surprise that I still do!). My love for reading began in my teenage years and my special interest was of memoirs. Much of my time (and money) was spent on my personal collection of books.

Hand-in-hand with reading is writing. Writing helped me understand the world as I see and experience it. Learning to touch-type as a young woman was hugely advantageous for me because, when typing, my fingers have a greater chance of keeping pace with my thoughts as they race through my brain.

So while some of my journals were handwritten (and for the most part, illegible!), much of it is typed and stored in password-protected files on USB sticks. (If this, too, is your preference, then I strongly recommend doing a back-up of your files every now and then).

I started typing one journal in 1999. Over a decade later, in 2010, I revisited that journal and added new experiences and thoughts I had learnt in the interval. Again, in 2020 and 2023, I revisited it again with even more insights and epiphanies. Looking back over that one journal now, spanning some 24 years, I can see how my understanding has evolved over a substantial period of time. It clearly shows how far I have come, even though it hasn't felt like that at times!

This is why I am so passionate about writing down the things that are important, and especially so in the context of grief and trauma. It helps us make sense of the senseless. It helps us process our memories over time. It preserves those memories. It provides us with a safe means for tapping into our thoughts, of expressing them, of giving them a voice.

Your loss may be recent or it may have occurred some time ago. It may have been your only pregnancy or perhaps you have experienced many pregnancy losses. Individually our experiences are unique to us, however, pregnancy loss can be a silent grief suffered by so many other couples, who, like you and me, had hoped to share their future with their precious little baby.

This, dear grieving parent, is my reason for writing this book for you. This book can be a safe place for you, where you can tell your own story of love and loss in your own words – and I, in turn, will also tell you a little of my story as well. I hope this will help you feel less alone in your experience. I hope it will help you feel understood and validated in this most traumatic event of your life.

Most of all, I hope that as time goes on, you will see that your grief is actually a beautiful expression of your love that keeps you emotionally connected to your sweet baby. He/she may no longer be in your arms, but they are safe in your heart and there you carry them with each brave step you take, every day, for the rest of your life.

Introduction

My Baby, My Grief, My Love (2025: 2nd Edn)

The inspiration for this book came from my earlier book, From One Twin Mum To Another: An insight into the complexities of multiple birth bereavement (2022). It has been written, first and foremost, for parents grieving the death of their baby. This book would also be insightful for anyone wanting to understand more about the grief of pregnancy loss; as well as being a valuable resource for health and mental health professionals who have grieving parents in their care.

Owing to the nature of pregnancy loss, both books contain similar themes and discussions. It is inevitable that there will be an overlap of ideas and concepts as both books are based on my personal experience, together with my observations and insights into the grief of twin loss and pregnancy loss respectively. However, each book is unique in it's own way and thus, they complement each other. I have endeavoured to keep the content of this book relevant to you, the reader.

Specifically, the three themes carried through both books are as follows:

Firstly, Chapter Two of my earlier book is called, "Your Grief (Your Love)". If I were to define grief using just one word, then that word would be LOVE. I truly believe that our grief is an expression of our love characterised by sadness and yearning. This personal definition of grief underscores much of what I say.

Secondly, I had included a list of writing prompts to help my readers explore their own experience of twin loss and grief in a meaningful way. Subsequently, those writing prompts have also inspired the concept for this book. I hope it provides you with a valuable opportunity to write about your grief in a safe and private place at this point of time.

Thirdly, I had also included a section on Self-Care and in Chapter Four of this book, I invite you to write your own self-care plan, exploring your own needs as you work through your grief, giving careful consideration for how those needs could be met.

It was over 20 years ago that I carried my twins, knowing that one of my babies had died and there was no guarantee that my surviving twin would be born alive. Whatever the circumstance of your pregnancy loss, I am so, so sorry you have to go through this trauma. The words I write in this book are for you. They are also the words I wish someone had thought to say to me all of those years ago.

I am writing this book with you in the forefront of my thinking. Through it's pages I want to reach out and reassure you, dear grieving parent, that you are not alone. Having my unborn twin die was not on my radar and I did not know of anyone anywhere in the world who'd had a twin pregnancy like mine. I felt all alone. I felt so misunderstood. I felt mentally unprepared for the journey that lay before me as I anticipated the birth of my twins.

Through the pages of this book, I also hope to reach out and reassure you that you will survive this. You will survive. Somehow, some way, you will summons the strength and resilience you need to grieve and come to terms with such a profound and devastating loss. It is not going to feel like this forever. I remember what it is like to be in those early days of grief. It is overwhelming and it is all-consuming. You do your best to get through one day at a time, sometimes even just one hour at a time.

Give yourself the time and space you need to grieve, and to grieve well. Your grief is, after all, a very special expression of your love.

With my love and thoughts for the journey you are on. Your loss is profound but you are not alone, for I am journeying alongside you.

With my warmest regards,

Julie Ann

A Note Regarding The Second Edition of This Book

After much thought I have elected to republish this book as a second edition with a few changes – the most notable of which are as follows:

1: The book width has decreased and thus, the dimensions are now at the more standard size of 216 x 140 mm.

2: The cover image has also changed to signify this new edition.

3: Intentionally short and concise, 36 of the 37 writing prompts can be viewed in their entirety on the open page.

3.1: The lined journalling pages in the originally published edition have been removed.

3.2: The subsequent rewording of: "How To Use This Book" consistent with the abovementioned change.

How To Use This Book

I wanted to keep the format of this book simple and clean.

There are, in total, 37 writing prompts spread over the four chapters of this book. In each one I briefly explore various aspects of grief in the context of pregnancy loss. Each prompt concludes with a question designed to help you write your own pregnancy loss journal.

As you read through the prompts, it may help to jot down a few important thoughts and memories and then express and explore your thoughts more fully using, for example, a writing pad or password-protected file on your computer. You may want to read through all of the prompts before you start writing (it could be helpful to do that chapter-by-chapter).

It may even be your preference to read the book through and leave the journalling part of it for now. This book will still be helpful in explaining grief as it relates to pregnancy loss and you can always come back to it again at a later time.

How you approach it is entirely up to you.

You may want to keep much of what you write private. There may be some things you'd like to share with your partner, a trusted friend, family member or grief counsellor.

Also remember there is no right or wrong thing to say, just whatever is right for you. Write whatever is in your heart.

It may help for you to use a writing technique called free association. This is where you write your thoughts unedited. Whenever a new thought pops into your mind, write it down. Don't question it, don't overthink it. It might feel a little disjointed and the thoughts may not seem to be relevant, however, just write it down anyway and keep on writing until you have absolutely nothing left to say. Then go back and read what you have written. It may surprise you the thoughts you have tapped into and it may give you new insights.

I hope that sharing a little of my journey will encourage you to tell your story in your own words, in your own way and that in doing so, a little peace will enter your heart.

Take Good Care Of You

By virtue of the fact that I have written this book, you will already know that I am passionate about writing. I am also a great believer in having good mental well-being. Writing is such good therapy when you are working through the process of grief and trauma, and we want to keep it that way!

However, it would be remiss of me to overlook the emotional aspect of remembering. There will be times when writing will be just what you need to do, as a part of telling your story and seeing your words, in your own handwriting, on the page in front of you.

Those words may help you cry. They may help you remember other things or understand your situation a little more deeply or differently. You may find it comforting and validating to see the story of your loss taking shape.

At other times your words may feel confronting and make you feel overwhelmed. If, at any point you do feel overwhelmed, it's okay to put your pen down and have a rest. This could help you keep it all at a manageable level.

There is no timeline for grief, so there is no need to rush your way through this journal. Take your time. You will come back to it again when you are ready, I promise!

Feeling overwhelmed may be a good indication to talk to someone in the meantime. It may be your partner, a trusted friend or family member; It may be your family doctor or another health or mental health professional, or perhaps even a Helpline telephone counsellor.

The key to taking good care of yourself is to be self-aware because then you will know what you need and you will have a better idea of how to meet those needs. Again, I mention the Self-Care Plan as outlined in Chapter Four, which I hope you will find beneficial.

If you have a history of prior mental illness, then it is good to be aware that it can coexist with your grief. Depression, for example, shares similar characteristics to grief, even though there are clear differences between the two. It is possible that clinical depression, for example, can recur concurrently with your grief, complicating and prolonging your grieving process.

When trying to conceive, or when a pregnancy loss occurs, our mental and emotional well-being is so important. You may already be under the care of a counsellor or psychologist and if they are made aware that you are struggling with your mental well-being, then extra help and support can be made available to you. I want to reassure you that there is no shame in struggling with your mental health, especially at a traumatic time like this.

It can be tempting to self-medicate grief, especially to aid sleeping or to numb the emotional pain. Please understand that this is not wise or helpful in the long-term and self-medicating with alcohol, over-the-counter, prescription or illicit drugs will only serve to complicate and prolong your grieving process. If this is an area of struggle for you, it would be far more beneficial to elicit extra support by talking to your family doctor or a mental health professional, preferably someone who understands pregnancy loss in the context of grief and trauma.

It can be hard enough navigating the daily pressures of life. Throw a trauma into the mix, such as experiencing pregnancy loss, and it is clear our need to be self-aware and to have strategies for coping is very important, as well as appropriate supports in place. Be self-aware and be diligent with your mental health because you deserve to feel well and to grieve well.

Now is a good opportunity to identify what health and mental health services are available to you in your local area and country. Your family doctor or other health/mental health professional may have already provided you with some contact details for peer and/or professional support. If you are unsure of what services are available to you in your local area, then I would encourage you to ask your family doctor.

On the following two pages, and for your future reference, spaces are provided for you to write some important contact details.

Contacts

Family Doctor:

Mental Health Professional:

National 24/7 Helpline/s:

Pregnancy Loss Support Group:

Other Important Contacts:

Chapter One:
My Baby

Your Sweet Baby Forever

I want to start by acknowledging your baby's humanity. Was your sweet baby a boy or a girl? If your loss was early and you're not sure, it is okay to go with your gut feeling. This is your baby.

You hold this book in your hands because you are grieving a life lost all too soon and that loss is profound. I am so sorry that you have to go through this heart-break. I know your loss is real. I know your grief is real. There is so much for you to process.

What did you name your baby? His/her name will belong to them forever, and I think that makes it very special. If you haven't already chosen a name for your baby, then I would encourage you to do so. I understand that this may be an emotionally difficult task. However, in a circumstance over which you had no control, this is the one thing you can control. Where so many things have already gone wrong, making this one decision will just feel right. Your baby's name will always be on your lips and to hear your son/daughter's name spoken out loud will always sound like the sweetest music to your ears.

Meggie was named in honour of the doctor who set me on the path to motherhood. Margaret is the English variant of the Celtic name Megan, and both names mean "pearl". After the birth, when I saw Meggie's tiny and frail but perfectly formed body, her skin was very pearl-like, which added to the significance and beauty of her name [i].

As well as naming your baby, a birth certificate is also an important acknowledgement of their existence. Here in Australia, when the loss isn't legally recognised as a stillbirth, parents can apply instead for a "Recognition of Early Pregnancy Loss" Certificate. I think this is a beautiful initiative and certainly, a very precious memento to keep. If you live outside of Australia, it might be worthwhile looking into if your country can provide you with something similar.

Tell Your Story ...

Is there a special significance for the name you have chosen for your baby?

Where It All Began

Let's go back to where it all began – your baby's conception.

Was this baby a planned pregnancy or did the news of your pregnancy come as a total surprise? If it was the latter, did the news of this pregnancy bring with it uncertainty for your future as you had planned it?

Do you fall pregnant easily? Or did you, like me, have a diagnosis of infertility and need the expertise of a reproductive gynaecologist to realise your dream of parenthood?

Was your baby conceived as a singleton? As a twin? As a higher-order multiple?

In the wider context, what else was going on in your life at that time? Were you studying? Were you working? What was that like for you as you mentally prepared yourself for pregnancy?

Life doesn't always happen in a linear fashion (as nice as that would be!) and you may have had other significant things going on at the time you fell pregnant. In that way the timing might not have been ideal and it's okay to have mixed feelings about that.

The news of your pregnancy may have had an impact on your relationship with your partner. Did it bring you closer together or was it a time of adjustment for you both?

My pregnancy was planned in that I was doing IVF, however, I would also describe it as "long awaited". It was 15 years leading up to the moment where I heard these words for the first time: "Congratulations, you are pregnant!" All of the pain and disappointment of so many years of primary infertility and failed treatment cycles just seemed to melt away in that instant.

As we adjust to being pregnant, the thought of a new life brings with it new hopes and dreams for our future and we start to imagine who this child will be and how they will fit into our family.

Tell Your Story ...

How did you feel when you learnt you were pregnant with this little one?

Your Pregnancy

Modern medical technology provides us with an insight into the most wonderfully complex inner world where our babies embark on their embryonic and fetal journey. Through my work as a radiology transcriptionist and as a former IVF patient, I have counted it a privilege to glimpse how amazing the human body is.

Pregnancy brings with it many changes as you prepare to welcome this new little life into your family. This can be a time filled with many emotions and it may take a while for you to mentally adjust to being pregnant.

On the one hand, you may feel well and truly ready for this new chapter of your life; On the other hand you may feel unprepared for the changes of pregnancy and of the challenges of parenthood.

Pregnancy is also a time of physical and hormonal change where your body accommodates this little person. There is no question that from a physical point of view, pregnancy can be quite exhausting.

While things were going well, did you sail through, feeling strong and healthy?

Or were you plagued with pregnancy-related issues such as morning (or all-day) sickness?

Were you given a prenatal diagnosis that left you with the heart-breaking decision to end the pregnancy on medical grounds?

Or did that prenatal diagnosis fill your days with appointments and the anxiety of having to deal with the unknown for the duration of the pregnancy?

If you have been pregnant before, your experience of this pregnancy will likely have been so different to before, both physically and mentally.

Tell Your Story ...

What was the pregnancy like for you?

In A Perfect World

I have always loved the sight of a pregnant woman. Pregnancy represents new life, it accommodates new life and it prepares for that new life to enter the world. When I see a pregnant woman, I think of her unborn baby – safe and protected.

We grow up understanding that there is the "natural order" to life in that we are born and we live to a ripe old age. We bring our children into the world, to love and protect them and wanting to be there to watch them grow up. As the years go by we welcome the next generation and we are also there to watch our children raise their own families.

Our children are meant to outlive us and in a perfect world, that's the way it would be. They are meant to be our future – they aren't supposed to die before we do.

Do you remember, as a child, adults asking you what you wanted to be when you grew up? Do you remember what you would say in reply? Even young children have a concept of what their future might look like.

As a young child, my answer was invariably: "I want to be a mum". The thought never entered my mind that I would (or could) be anything else. That is what my perfect world looked like. I would be a mother and my children would be my greatest achievement in life.

With the benefit of hindsight, I can see that many of the big decisions through my life as a young woman were influenced by this single-minded desire. It influenced the jobs I worked, the doctors I saw, commencing the long process of investigating a clear cause for my infertility, marrying my husband and undergoing IVF... It was all because I wanted to be a mother and it never occurred to me that I would outlive any of my babies.

Tell Your Story ...

What about you – what did your perfect world look like?

The Day Everything Changed Forever

The one thing I have noticed about pregnancy loss is that every couple will have that one day that stands out in their memory as the day everything changed forever. They will always be able to recall the events of that day because some details are etched into their memories.

For me, it was at the mid-pregnancy ultrasound.

Despite the uncomfortably full bladder, I was buzzing with excitement as I arrived for my appointment... The sonographer explained everything to us as he went along. We saw our precious Twin A's brain, eyes, fingers and toes, stomach, bladder, heart and spine. We were given such a wonderful glimpse of our little boy.

I was just quietly marvelling at everything we had seen so far when the sonographer looked at me and said, "Julie, I don't know how to tell you this but your Twin B is a lot smaller than Twin A." It took a few moments for his words to sink in. When I asked, "can you see a heartbeat?", I instinctively already knew the answer. He said he couldn't and that he was really sorry and went to consult with the radiologist.

I was in disbelief that one of my babies had died. I have since replayed that moment over in my mind a thousand times and each time I think nothing can prepare you for being told that your baby is dead [ii].

That day marked the end of the "BEFORE" where I had felt so very healthy and happy, blissfully unaware that anything was wrong.

It also marked the beginning of the "AFTER" where my twin pregnancy became "high-risk and complicated" and I embarked on a long and anxious journey of navigating my way through an unknown world, mentally preparing myself for the full-term live birth and stillbirth of my twins.

Tell Your Story ...

What happened that sad day for you?
What was it like from then on?

The First Of Many Goodbyes

Whilst still pregnant, we may start to develop a strong emotional bond with our baby. This may begin the moment we learn we are pregnant, or it might develop over time.

If your pregnancy was more advanced, you may have had a funeral for your baby and this will have been an important opportunity for family and friends to gather around and support your grief for such a profound loss. It is also perhaps the only opportunity many in your various social circles will have to make an emotional connection with your baby.

Sadly, we didn't get to have a funeral for Meggie and lay her to rest as we would have liked. This is my biggest regret. In coming to terms with this significant missed opportunity, I have realised over the years that there are many goodbyes that we will say to our babies.

There may be one main goodbye such as at the funeral, however, many more goodbyes will follow through the years. Every grieving parent will have to say goodbye to the missed opportunity to parent their child, and for their son/daughter to live and grow and learn and experience life.

Other goodbyes may occur on your baby's due date, his/her birthday, anniversaries and special days, and other significant occasions in your family. It may be the special milestones your baby will miss.

At these times, each goodbye provides you with another opportunity to acknowledge your baby's humanity and of his/her ongoing place within your family and in your heart. These goodbyes may feel, at times, beautiful or heart-breaking or bittersweet.

I hope they also bring a measure of comfort and peace to know that you will always carry your baby in your heart and in that way, he/she will never leave you.

Tell Your Story ...

What goodbyes have you needed to say?

What Has Helped You To "Hang On"?

You observe the world quite differently when you are in acute grief. You wonder how everyone else can go about their daily lives when your baby has died. The loss feels overwhelming. You may feel like your heart has actually broken in two.

Just as discovering you are pregnant brings with it a new focus, so too does losing that pregnancy. This little baby was already important in your life. Despite the feeling that everything has changed forever, bravely you keep going, one step at a time. You start to realise within yourself an inner strength, a resilience and courage that, until now, you hadn't known you were capable of. You may not feel strong or resilient, but you are.

You may not have gone through anything like pregnancy loss before, but you have possibly experienced other circumstances of loss. What helped you cope then? Could that coping mechanism help equip you now through this deeply traumatic time? As I write, a few more questions have popped into my mind, as follows:

- Do you have a belief system that helps sustain you?

- Is it the hope that happier days will follow after this sad season of your life?

- Is there someone in your circles who will "get it" with your grief and will always remember your baby with you?

- Do you have that one special person who gives you the time and space to cry?

- Is there a special interest or hobby that helps you express your grief? Or perhaps it provides you with a reprieve from the intensity of your grief?

- Do you have a hope in your heart that one day you will be brave to try to conceive again?

Tell Your Story ...

What has your experience of loss taught you about yourself and helped you hang on?

A Sweet Memory

Despite the profound loss of our baby Meggie, there were still some beautiful memories of the pregnancy. Those memories helped me "hang on" through those long weeks of mentally preparing myself for the birth of my twins.

Going through the intensity of grief your mind is focused predominantly on the sadness and then something beautiful happens to remind you that there are still moments that will bring you happiness. I want to reassure you that it is okay to enjoy those moments.

When in acute grief we often have a tendency to feel guilty about enjoying the things that would normally make us smile, however, that enjoyment helps provide a balance to our feelings and we need that for our mental well-being.

Here is one memory that is especially dear to my heart:

It was Mother's Day and we had gone to our local boat harbour early that morning to release a dozen pink roses into the ocean and watch the sunrise. My husband and I walked to the end of the wharf and sat on the step with the water lapping at our feet.

One by one we placed the roses into the water and watched, mesmerised by the shimmering ocean, as each rose floated away. We couldn't help but notice, however, that one rose stayed in the water at our feet, even when we had lost sight of all the others. At that time, I was a few weeks off giving birth to my twins and I took great comfort in that one little rose. It was almost as if Meggie was letting us know she will never leave us, that she will always be with us.

The sunrise that Sunday morning was especially beautiful and memorable. It should come as no surprise that every morning I love to watch the sky as I slowly wake up. It's the one time of the day when I can just be quiet with my thoughts and spend some time with Meggie.

Tell Your Story ...

What memory of your pregnancy makes you smile, albeit through the tears?

Perfect In Every Way

The work of the late Swedish photographer, Lennart Nilsson, has always held a great fascination for me. His inutero photography provides a glimpse into that complex inner world where life begins for us all. Whilst pregnant with my twins, I often looked online to see fetal images at a similar gestation to my surviving twin. Similarly, I also saw amazing fetal images the same size that Meggie was while she was still alive. I found it very reassuring to see how perfectly formed these little babies were.

For the second half of my twin pregnancy, I was monitored very closely. I had regular obstetric ultrasounds to check on my surviving twin's growth and well-being, as well as to check that the separating membrane between the two gestational sacs remained intact. I would always try to memorise what Meggie looked like on the ultrasound screen, never quite sure if this would be the last time I would see her.

As my surviving twin grew inutero, Meggie's tiny body was compressed high up against the uterine wall. I always found comfort in knowing she was positioned just under my heart and that while she was still alive, her little heart beat just under mine.

However, as I approached full-term and was anticipating the birth of my twins, I became very anxious and fearful of what Meggie might look like, acutely aware that she had died several weeks before.

The morning of my twins births, the midwives reassured my husband and I that Meggie would always be our sweet little baby and that she would be perfect in every way. And she was.

Meggie was so tiny that she was the same size as my hand. Despite her small size, she was perfectly formed. We could see her fingers, her toes, and the vertebrae of her spine. How could we not marvel at this perfect little miracle?

Tell Your Story ...

Did you get to see your baby?

Did he/she have any endearing features that are a precious memory for you?

If you didn't see your baby, how do you imagine him/her?

Chapter Two:
My Grief

The Process Of Grief

I often say that grief is not optional. As hard as it is, grief is a necessary and healthy process that allows you to feel the pain of acknowledging your baby has died and of courageously finding your way forward in the face of this heart-breaking loss.

Personally, I believe that the grieving process is far more complex than the various "stage" theories that have emerged through the decades. Furthermore, I believe that the process of grief that you experience will be unique to you – just as your personality and other life experiences are unique to you. Your grief will be influenced by the emotional connection you have already developed with your baby. It will also be influenced by how supported you feel as you grieve this loss.

In those early days you will need time and space to process your loss, to process the trauma and all of the emotions and memories that are associated with your pregnancy. As time goes on, you will find a place for those emotions and the memories, and they won't feel as intense or raw as they do right now.

I want to reassure you that there is no right or wrong way to grieve, just so long as your grief is expressed in a healthy and safe way, and that you feel the support from others is adequate for you and your needs. Whatever it is that feels natural to you and aligns with what you believe, that's what you will need to do. Cry when you need to, you need those tears. It's okay to laugh as well, don't feel guilty about that. Give yourself permission to feel whatever you need to at any given moment.

Grief doesn't exist within the confines of time and I want to encourage you to grieve for as long as you need to. You will know that you have grieved well because, after having found a place for your memories and emotions, you will feel more at peace with your grief.

Tell Your Story ...

How would you describe the process of grief, as you have experienced it?

You Feel Sad, Just So Sad

In it's simplest form, grief is love that is characterised by sadness and yearning. It leaves you feeling sad, just so sad. Sadness is a natural and very understandable response to the loss you have experienced.

In trying to help others understand why pregnancy loss is so painful, I explain it in this way: When a baby dies, the parents lives have changed forever. The future they had already started to imagine, with this child as an important part of it, has changed. That leaves them with having to find a way to reconcile the future they thought they had with the future they now have. This realisation evokes deep feelings of sadness and our tears are a natural expression of that deep sadness.

When we express our sadness through crying, our tears contain oxytocin. This endorphin helps us cope with stress and can bring some relief to our emotional pain. This is why it is really important to cry for as long as we need and only stop when we feel we are ready.

Have you noticed that grief makes you feel almost child-like again? Grief puts us in a position of needing to be comforted and looked after. We also need to be heard and feel reassured. We need to know that the depth of our sadness is understood.

Anyone in a supporting role needs to understand that it isn't comforting to stop us from crying, but rather to allow us to cry, lovingly and gently holding that space for us. Those in a supporting role also need to understand that we are not attention-seeking or being self-indulgent when we cry... We are grieving and we are sad, just so sad.

That sadness will stay with us for as long as we need to feel it and not only is sadness an understandable response to our loss, but it is also healthy to express it.

Tell Your Story ...

Is there someone who has been there for you, who has sat with you in your sadness and given you the time and emotional safety to cry?

And You Feel So Many Other Things As Well

Sadness is, perhaps, the one emotion that we will automatically associate with grief; However, it is not the only one. Not only have you lost your future, but you may also feel the loss of social recognition as the parent of your child.

You may feel robbed of something so precious, having to pack up your baby's belongings, packing up your baby's life before it had even begun.

Those early days of grief come with an overwhelming sense that everything has happened outside of your ability to control and this may leave you feeling helpless and vulnerable.

Grieving can also leave you feeling isolated if your extended circles don't understand the depth of your loss and grief. Now more than ever, you need to feel understood and validated, and for your grief to be accepted and supported.

You may feel the pressure to put on a "brave face" and just get on with life in an effort to make others feel comfortable about being around you (be mindful that it's not your job to do that for them). This pressure could feel very premature given how raw your grief is in the early days.

Through all of your grief and sadness, there is an overwhelming sense that things should have been very different. Your baby's death was intensely unfair and senseless. Your grief and trauma may be expressed as anger and, given the circumstances, anger is very understandable for the deep emotional pain you are experiencing. There will always be a valid reason for why you feel the way you do (and we will explore this more later in the Self-Care Plan).

It is important to allow yourself to feel all of your emotions in a safe and manageable way, as difficult and crushing as they are. Remember what I said in "Take Good Care Of You" and to reach out for extra support when you need it.

Tell Your Story ...

Is there a difficult emotion you are struggling with at the moment?

The Questions Grief Asks

The death of a baby can leave us questioning many things. These questions will be confronting and perplexing. It may leave us questioning the meaning of life. We may challenge, for the first time in our life, the beliefs we have always held. We will likely go over and over these questions in our mind, "Why did this happen to us? Why did our baby have to die?"

There may be questions for which there will be no easy answer (or perhaps no answers at all) and one of the most difficult parts of grieving is that somehow, some way, some time, we need to come to a place of acceptance with or without those answers.

As you know, I carried my twin baby dead for the second half of my first IVF pregnancy. When I fell pregnant through our second IVF, I had a subchorionic bleed resulting in the early miscarriage of our twin embryo, however, that pregnancy continued to full-term without any further complications.

Having already had a 15-year-long journey through infertility to become pregnant, and then to experience twin loss with both pregnancies, served to reinforce that unsettling feeling that time-and-time again my body had let me down.

I felt guilty for not being able to protect my unborn babies. I felt guilty for not realising that Meggie had died. My grief tormented me with the question: "Was it something I did (or didn't) do?"

It took a long time to accept that I wasn't personally responsible for the death of my unborn babies and to come to a place of peace within myself.

I understand how these feelings can persist and torment you, even when logically you know that there was not a single thing you could have done to change the outcome. Because you and I both know that the truth is: if you could have, you would have.

Tell Your Story ...

What questions is your grief asking?

Those Sleepless Nights

Working your way through those difficult emotions and feelings of helplessness, guilt and anger, etc, can have a huge impact on your sleeping. Despite the emotional and physical exhaustion, sleep doesn't come easily with grief and trauma. Tossing and turning and going over it all in your mind, knowing you need the sleep, can be hugely frustrating.

Dreaming is another way that our mind works through grief, and our dreams can also leave us lying awake afterwards. Grief dreams are often of yearning and searching. You will remember some dreams with clarity, while others will seem perplexing. Some dreams may bring with them a measure of peace, whilst others will leave you feeling confused or rattled. Using the free association technique mentioned in "How To Use This Book" may help make sense of your dream.

Much of my wakeful hours through those long nights of grief were spent trying to process the memories of my twin pregnancy and the birth, both of which were very traumatic experiences. My journals became my constant companion as, one-by-one, my fragmented memories resurfaced and, rather like putting together a huge jigsaw puzzle, I was able to find a place for each memory, one jigsaw piece at a time.

At the beginning of this book, spaces were provided for you to write down helpful phone numbers available to you. If you find that night-times are the hardest to get through, where it seems everyone is asleep except for you, then it might be reassuring to talk to someone. The 24/7 helplines are there for that reason. Whilst the telephone counsellor won't know you personally, they will likely have a good sense of the emotional support you are needing in that moment. Taking that brave step of reaching out in your moment of need may be one of the best things you can do for yourself. Their words could help guide you through a very difficult time.

Tell Your Story ...

What thoughts keep you awake at night?

Time Stands Still
But Life Doesn't Wait

I remember in those very early days of my loss wondering how the world could continue on as though nothing had happened. It felt like I was in a shop-front, frozen in time, watching the world outside continue on, passing me by.

Following a loss, it takes a long time to summons the energy you need to rejoin the outside world once again. However, your own personal circumstances may leave you with no choice but to merge back into the fast lane of life again, even though right now you feel so emotionally unprepared for it.

On top of all of the difficult emotions and feelings to navigate, pregnancy loss can occur after successful pregnancies and you may have other living children to care for and support through their grief as well. This will also mean that they will have their own established routines, for example, with attending school and perhaps also after-school activities. There will be meals to cook and laundry to do and bedtime stories to read.

Your living children may be too young to articulate their understanding of the circumstance or they may need you to explain it to them in an age-appropriate way. In this way, you will be helping them navigate their grief as well as navigating your own.

People will often say "let me know if you need anything" and this is perhaps an indication that they will wait for you to make that first move. However, in early grief it can be quite difficult to say what your needs are. It is often more helpful when people offer to do something specific, such as the school runs or take your children for a few hours so that you can rest. Or they may, at a time that is mutually convenient, drop off ready-made meals so that becomes one less thing for you to do at the end of the day.

Tell Your Story ...

What practical help from family and friends would you really appreciate?

Complex Grief, Simple Needs

I am guessing you have days where your grief feels like a tangled mess. I know I did. And within that tangled mess, you realise that there is nothing linear about the process of grieving. Yes, the intensity of it will lessen with time, but you also have to allow your grief to be felt and experienced in a way that comes naturally to you.

Remember, the process of grief for each of us is unique and individual, in the same way that our personality and life experiences are unique to us. When we peel back all of the layers of our grief and trauma, and of what makes it so unique and complex for us, we will find at the core that our needs are often very simple.

We need to be heard and validated.
We need to feel understood and empowered.

In acute grief, we need to tell our story of loss over and over. There is power in hearing our words, our thoughts, our memories, spoken out loud. This can be helpful in making sense of our loss and trauma. We need to know that the person we are sharing our grief with "gets it". They get that our loss is real, our grief is real. When someone conveys to us that they understand what we are saying, we feel validated, we feel strengthened. It is empowering. When we feel their support around us, it is because we also feel understood.

In the wider context, the experience of the loss itself was outside of our ability to control and that makes feeling supported and empowered all the more important. Having the right people around you can help facilitate that. We have many interpersonal relationships and just as different people will have different roles in our lives, they will also meet different needs and that could be helpful as you adjust to the long-term "new normal" of your life. One day you will enable your own coping mechanisms once again and you will get there with the right support around you.

Tell Your Story ...

What do you need from those around you with regards to your grief?

Those "What If" Moments

I think every grieving person has felt the pressure to deal with the practical, day-to-day busyness of life before they are ready. At times we may be doing okay and then another wave of grief washes over us. Once again we find ourselves wondering what might have been. It might be a memory or perhaps something someone says that catches us off guard.

Some "what if" moments will torment us. "What if I had done this... or that? What if this had happened... or what if that hadn't happened?" I know this is much, much easier said than done, but we do have to be ever so gentle and kind to ourselves when dealing with the unknowns of our situation. Again, some questions about our loss and grief will arise for which there will not be an answer.

If you have living children you will watch them grow and reach milestones and those "what if" moments may leave you struggling once again with those unanswered questions of your loss.

It may be that your living child has a little playmate who bears the same name as your baby.

It may be that a friend or relative was also pregnant at the same time as you and you observe quietly from the sidelines as things go well for them.

It is very understandable when watching your living child and those in your extended circles, that you will have those moments of wondering "what if".

In those "what if" conversations with other grieving parents, I have often sensed that they are an expression of our love and our yearning for all of the missed opportunities for our baby to live and experience life, and for us and our living children to bear witness to that and to experience life with them.

I consider those "what if" moments as our grief saying, "I miss you… I wish you were here."

Tell Your Story …

What are those "what if" moments like for you?

If Your Living Child Is A Surviving Twin

Perhaps your living child was born one of twins (or a higher-order multiple). With multiple birth bereavement, there is an added layer of complexity because as grieving parents, you are living with two simultaneous realities – on the one hand, you are caring for your surviving twin's needs around-the-clock and on the other hand, you are grieving for your baby twin who has died.

It is my experience that the grief of twin loss is often overlooked because the sight of a mother cradling a baby in her arms isn't an image we normally associate with grief and loss. Furthermore, the grieving parents are often encouraged to focus on their surviving twin and, at the same time, discouraged from grieving the death of their baby twin.

Some people apologised for congratulating me on my twin pregnancy. Others told me to be happy I still have one baby... And to think positively... I am sure you can imagine how these words came across as cruel as I mentally prepared myself for both a live birth and a stillbirth (and the possibility of two stillbirths).

After my twins were born others misinterpreted my grief, asking: How would you have coped with two babies? (Sadly, I never got to know.)

Again, with a surviving twin, there will be those "what if" moments as you watch your child grow, experience life and reach milestones and, on account of this, of having a clear idea of where your baby twin would be age-wise and developmentally. And all the while you know that your surviving twin is navigating life without their womb-mate and that, as they grow in their own awareness of themselves as a twinless twin, you will play a huge ongoing role in supporting them through their own feelings of loss and of their sense of self.

If you are a twin mother like me, my first book **From One Twin Mum To Another** was written for you. It takes an in-depth look at what sets twin loss apart from other types of pregnancy loss.

Tell Your Story ...

What would you like people to understand about your twins and your grief?

Your Partner

Just as your experience of grief will be unique to you, so too will that of your partner. Whilst at the very heart of grief for you both is love, sadness and yearning, the way that grief is expressed could be quite different. It may even feel that your respective grieving processes are out-of-sync.

One partner may actively elicit emotional support by joining a pregnancy loss peer support group. There they will openly recount their story of loss, meeting their need to tell their story over and over, and identifying with others who share similar stories.

The other partner may seek the company of just one or two close friends, or perhaps even prefer solitude. They may express their grief in a physical way, such as through exercise or sport. Or they may seek emotional intimacy and comfort through sex.

One partner may feel unable to function in their everyday life. The other partner may throw themselves into their work or study.

We each have our own "default" setting for coping and adjusting to life in the face of our loss. The grief that we feel inside won't always be obvious to others, even though it is there and it is felt very deeply. It is therefore important to understand and respect that there will be differences in how each partner expresses their grief and to lean on one another for understanding and support. Always be mindful that you are in this together as a couple even though you will work through your grief as individuals.

Remember that grief is an intuitive process and it will be expressed in a way that feels natural, individual and personal. And so long as that expression is healthy and does no harm to yourself or anyone else, then there is no right or wrong way to grieve.

Tell Your Story ...

What can you do for your partner that will make a difference to their healing?

Who You Are Because Of Your Grief

There are parts about your personality that are innately you, things that likely won't change over time. When we experience loss and the subsequent grieving process a part of us, however, does change forever. While the grief is acute, it is all-consuming. It may leave you wondering, "Who am I now?" or "Who am I becoming?".

You may have a strong sense of lost innocence and remember those days when everything was going so well. It didn't even enter your mind of what you were about to experience. You remember the way it used to be and you miss that innocence. You really miss the old you, your non-grieving self.

You wonder how long you are going to feel this way and if things are ever going to feel normal again. It may worry you about falling pregnant again and losing another baby. Or you may have experienced pregnancy loss before and wonder if you will ever have a living baby.

You may feel anxious about who you would be without children to satisfy your maternal instincts. I remember those long years of primary infertility and of how compellingly strong my desire was to fall pregnant, even as I was forced to consider the possibility of remaining childless.

Looking through the lens of loss, the world does look different now. It has changed because your baby is no longer a part of your future. Not only that, the way you look at life has also changed. Loss and grief is now your lived experience.

Working through the process of grief, you will settle into a new normal and one day you will feel more like your old self again, only now you have a deeper understanding of life and loss and love. Through your lived experience, you have a greater appreciation for how fragile life can be but also of how precious life is.

Tell Your Story ...

What would you tell your younger self about the experience of loss and grief?

What does this new world look like for you?

What Was Helpful At The Time Of Your Loss

I am aware that there are various aspects of what is helpful because, on the one hand, there is the medical care provided to you and on the other hand, there are your social circles of family and friends.

Often the initial point of contact at the time of your loss will be your family doctor and you may have been admitted into hospital, receiving care from other health professionals. I believe the large majority of health and mental health professionals in their chosen fields want to provide the best care they can.

Whilst in their care you may have been given opportunities for memory-making with your baby. They may have linked you into additional professional support, such as grief counselling, or perhaps a local peer support group. There may have been one nurse or doctor who was especially kind towards you at that time.

When news of your loss filters through to your social circles, many people will share in your sadness. They may reach out, sending a text message or email, or perhaps leave a handwritten note in your letterbox. Some may share their own experience of pregnancy loss with you to provide some reassurance that you are not alone.

You may run into an old friend in the shopping centre and the rekindling of the friendship at this time means the world to you.

People close to you will rally at times like this, wanting to offer practical help, and you will appreciate the kindness they extend to you. And you will always remember their kindness with a deep sense of gratitude.

Tell Your Story ...

What stands out as being especially helpful at the time of your loss?

However, Not Everything Is Helpful

Sadly, there is a flip-side to what we find helpful at the time of our loss. Even with good intentions, some people may do or say things that are really unhelpful. There was a lot of nervous energy surrounding my twin pregnancy and not everyone got it right. Some things served to complicate and prolong my grieving process and added, what I call, layers of unnecessary grief.

Personally, I think one of the more complicated aspects regarding the grief of pregnancy loss is dealing with the reactions of other people (and we will continue to explore this more in the next writing prompt as well).

Not everybody will understand or try to empathise with our circumstance of loss. It seems we each will have that "horror story" of something someone said to us, a careless remark that they possibly won't recall later, though we will feel the sting of their words for a long, long time.

I found that these unhelpful encounters presented me with a quandary. It is easier said than done to walk away and forget about the conversation. It can be unhelpful to ruminate it over in your mind. And forgiving the person is a big ask. The measure I use is to determine what my relationship with this person means to me. If they are important in my life, then I would have to find a way to free myself from the pain their words or actions have caused me. However, I would do this in my own way, in my own time and on my own terms.

I think it is really important to rely on our gut instincts regarding people. Whilst we will have a strong sense of emotional safety with some people, we will similarly have a strong sense that we can't trust others with the more private details of our loss. People may ask about our loss out of curiosity, but they may not be that safe place we need at a time when we are already feeling quite vulnerable. They may even make us feel violated – and our gut feeling will tell us that.

Tell Your Story ...

What did you find unhelpful at the time of your loss?

What layers of unnecessary grief have you experienced?

Those Tricky Conversations

As mentioned in the previous prompt, it is not easy navigating some of the reactions that others have towards our loss. Some people will default to clichés, often without any self-awareness or insight into how hurtful and cruel their words are. Many clichés were quoted at me, such as, "Don't worry, dear, you can always have another one... Miscarriages are natures mistakes... It wasn't a baby anyway... It wasn't meant to be... Your baby is in a better place... Everything happens for a reason..." and the list goes on.

Those comments always left me feeling hurt and misunderstood in my grief because, even pre-loss, it would not have occured to me to make such comments to anyone else in a similar situation. It was confronting to hear those things being said to me.

Even having a curious stranger ask, "How many children do you have?" presents us with the dilemma of what to say and how to say it. On the one hand, we feel guilty for not mentioning our baby who has died but on the other hand, to mention him/her leaves us vulnerable to how that person might react. They may react with kindness and care, or they may not understand our grief and say something that leaves us feeling wounded and disempowered.

Over the years, I have learnt to always, always rely on my gut feeling about the person I am talking to. I ask myself, "How do I feel about them and this conversation?".

If there is any hint of a doubt in my mind and I sense the emotional safety isn't there, then I will protect Meggie by not mentioning her. I am also protecting myself and I think this is really important when it comes to how vulnerable we can be in some social situations.

There is that well-known idiom, "Don't throw your pearl to the swine" and I think that it is also applicable here. We need to be discerning about people. We need to protect and empower ourselves. And we need to protect the memory of our baby.

Tell Your Story ...

How have you navigated those tricky conversations?

What Would You Like Other Grieving Parents To Know?

There's a saying that when you experience pregnancy loss, you become a member of the club that nobody chooses to join. You know from your own experience how traumatic it is to lose your precious baby. You now know about things that you had been oblivious to previously.

Through your experience of loss and trauma, you now have first-hand knowledge and understanding of what other couples in similar circumstances have also gone through. In a very real sense your understanding goes beyond empathy. You don't have to try to imagine what it would be like because you already know. You know. It is your lived experience. No matter how much time goes by, you will always remember what that grief feels like and because of that you will be better able to convey your genuine observations and insights into the nature of grief.

Following a loss, we may fall into the role of educating those around us about our grief. With other newly bereaved parents, it is different. We don't have to educate them because, like us, they know. However, as the years go by and we mentally process more of our experience of grief, we gain new insights and understanding into the nature of grief. As time goes by, that insightful and discerning wisdom you have acquired could be just what newly bereaved parents need to hear, especially as their loss and trauma is very recent and raw.

Talking to them about grief and conveying that they are not alone could make the world of difference to how they grieve. I'm pretty sure they will know you "get it" and that you will help them feel understood and validated in the pain they are experiencing.

They would see that grief – as heart-breaking as it is – is survivable and that it is not going to feel this raw forever. You may be that one person who understands how important it is to sit with them in their sadness, giving them the time and space they need in that moment.

Tell Your Story ...

If you had a chance to talk to newly bereaved parents, what would you say to them?

Chapter Three:

My Love

My Grief, My Love

Just a few weeks after my loss, I remember being scolded for not "being over it" yet. The words spoken to me that day left me feeling quite upset. Grief isn't something to be frowned upon, and it's not like a head cold or stomach bug that we'll get over in a few days.

Yes, I will say it again: Our grief is our love, our sadness and our yearning all wrapped up in the unseen but meaningful connection we have already developed with our unborn baby. The deep feelings of grief are powerful and all-consuming. Our grief is a very understandable response to the profound loss we have experienced. Our arms may ache from the feelings of emptiness. Our heart may feel like it has actually broken in two. We need to be gentle and kind to ourselves as we embark on the journey of healing from the trauma.

I have often said that we can't not grieve. Grief has a way of demanding our attention and, as crushing and painful as it is, it is necessary for our long-term mental well-being to grieve in a way that comes naturally to us. Our grief has to be felt. It deserves to be expressed.

In the absence of our baby we carry them in our grief, in our love. They have their own special place within our heart and there they will forever remain. When we understand grief in the context of love, we will see that over time it becomes a beautiful expression of our ongoing love. It is because of our love that the emotional connection that we have with our baby will continue to grow stronger and even more meaningful with each passing year.

There will always be a touch of sadness when you think of your baby, however, as time goes by and the intense pain lessens, you will know you have grieved well because some peace has entered into your heart.

Tell Your Story ...

What does your grief look like?

A Special Place For Remembering

You may have just a few tangible reminders of your baby. It may be an ultrasound image very early on, when the viability of your pregnancy was confirmed. You may have bought or been gifted with a sweet item of clothing, a baby blanket or a teddy bear; Something that now, whenever you look at it, is symbolic of your baby. The things belonging to your baby may be few, but they are so very precious.

You may have already set up the nursery, considering all that you will need to accommodate this new little person in your family. You may have been ready to bring your baby home and now you face the heart-breaking task of packing it all up.

Memorialising is also an important part of grief and of finding a place for your baby's things. There is something special about having a tangible memento, something that you can hold in your hands and feel, to look at, to smell, to hold against your cheek. Perhaps you have a shelf displaying a few photos, figurines, candles or anything that you associate with your baby.

You may have a Memory Box which contains precious mementos for you to look at whenever you need to. It may also contain handwritten cards received at the time of your loss.

You may have a favourite room with a peaceful view or a section in your garden with your favourite flowers where you can sit and take in some sunshine and fresh air, and just be alone with your thoughts.

You may feel drawn to visit a place that means something special to you.

Earlier we talked about the pressure to rush back into our daily routines and we don't always have the luxury to choose. However, when we need to, and whenever we can, we have that one place we can go to just sit still, to remember and be with our grief.

Tell Your Story ...

Do you have a special place for your babies things?

Is there a special place where you can "just be" with your grief?

Give Your Love A Memory

As a way of honouring your baby's life and humanity, you might want to do something special in their memory. With time, you may find great therapy in having a creative outlet for expressing your grief, for telling your story of loss.

It may be using a talent that you have already developed through the years, or perhaps you might want to try something new. It might be putting together a photo album or scrapbook, creating an artwork, or compiling a playlist of songs that bring you comfort. You might write a poem, or perhaps even lyrics for a song, about your baby. Whatever you do, it will make your heart swell with pride and it will always be a beautiful reminder of your baby.

Some people find great personal meaning in making a donation in their baby's memory. It might be to an organisation that you hold in high regard and one which offers help to other people in their time of great need.

There are so many beautiful things that you can do to give your love a memory and you will find that over the years, you will be giving your love many beautiful memories. I know it will never be the same as making memories with your child had they lived, however, you are doing something positive and empowering that, bit-by-bit helps a little more peace enter into your heart.

Several years ago my husband gave me a DSLR camera and suggested I take a class to learn how to use it manually.

I have always enjoyed photography and this thoughtful gift opened up a whole new world for me. Over the years I have taken hundreds of photos of roses and raindrops. The roses represent the beauty and fragility of Meggie and the raindrops represent my love and tears. I am not the most artistic person, so it brings my heart so much joy to use the camera to create something so beautiful and meaningful. This is my way of giving my love a memory.

Tell Your Story ...

How can you give your love a memory that will mean the world to you through the years?

Your Baby's Special Day

Is there a day you have set aside to honour your baby's memory? It may be your baby's birth day, or perhaps the anniversary of their death or funeral. It could even be the anniversary of your obstetric ultrasound or any other day that has great personal meaning for you and your partner.

With each passing year, this day will take on greater significance and meaning because of your ongoing love for your baby.

It may be a day that you want to share with others or you might prefer to keep it quiet and private, a day where you can just be you with your grief and memories.

It would be a good opportunity to do something specific, such as taking a bunch of flowers to the Memorial Gardens to lay at your baby's plaque or headstone.

You might want to set aside some time to listen to a special playlist of songs or write a love-letter to your baby.

It will always be a day tinged with sadness (remember, your grief is your love). As the years go by and that sadness isn't quite so intense, this day will become all the more special because you have given your love so many beautiful memories in honour of your baby. With the sadness there will also be beauty and, I genuinely hope, there will be moments that you will remember with a smile.

You may also find that some years, your baby's special day will pass quietly and peacefully. But on other years, your feelings and memories will feel raw all over again. It is very normal for grief to ebb and flow in this way. When I have experienced those harder days, I find it helpful to remember that gentler days will follow.

Again, there is no right or wrong way to approach your baby's special day, just whatever feels right for you and your partner.

Tell Your Story ...

What would be meaningful for you to do on your baby's special day?

Other Family-Oriented Days

Following a loss, there will be other important days to navigate and it is good to consider how you might approach those days as well. They may be significant days within your household, such as family birthdays and anniversaries. Alternatively, they may occur in the context of your wider family – days like Mothers Day, Fathers Day, Christmas, Easter, and any other family-oriented occasions in your extended circles that you would normally participate in.

You may also find, while your grief is raw, that the expectations others have of you may not align with your own expectations for now. You might feel the pressure to be outwardly happy and celebrate these occasions with everyone else.

It may be about finding a balance to participate in those other family-oriented occasions so that you can keep it all at a manageable level for yourself. There may be someone who you know will look out for you and it might be helpful to touch base with them in advance. You might also find it helpful to go just for an hour or so, and give yourself permission to leave when the time feels right for you.

You might find great comfort in wearing a piece of jewellery in your baby's memory. My favourite pendant on a chain is infinity-shaped with the inscription "Always In My Heart" and I find great comfort in the thought that Meggie is symbolically there with me too.

Your grief will change and evolve as the years go by and it isn't always going to be so raw, but while it is you will need to be self-aware of what you can – and can't – cope with at the moment. Good self-care makes it okay to say no to those things you can't cope with for now.

It will be empowering for you to consider how to approach social occasions going forward. This is especially true if any of those other occasions occur close to your baby's special day.

Tell Your Story ...

What do you need those in your extended circles to understand about your grief?

Your Own Traditions

Creating your own traditions is another way that you can give your love a memory. Traditions serve as an ongoing way of affirming your baby's place within your family. It may be something that is culturally meaningful for you and your family. Listed below are a few thoughts:

- There may be a special ornament that you hang on the Christmas tree each year.

- Your local Memorial Gardens may hold an annual memorial service for you to attend.

- The International Bereaved Mothers Day occurs annually on the first Sunday of May.

- The International Bereaved Fathers Day occurs annually on the last Sunday of August.

- October is recognised around the world as Pregnancy and Infant Loss Awareness Month and many online events are held throughout the month.

- 15 October is observed annually as Pregnancy and Infant Loss Awareness Day.

- 7pm on 15 October is the International Wave of Light where – in your time zone, no matter where you are in the world – you are invited to light a candle in your baby's memory.

You may have other ideas for traditions you can create in honour of your baby. For any hand-written cards, when I sign our names I always include a little love-heart with an M inside it to signify Meggie's place within our family. It makes my heart feel good to affirm her in this way.

Everything that you do, no matter how big or small, to memorialise your baby will hold great personal meaning for you and it will strengthen your emotional connection to him/her. When you create your own traditions to carry on through the years, you know that your baby will always have their special place inside your heart and within your family.

Tell Your Story ...

Are there traditions you would like to create in honour of your baby?

Love-Letter To Your Baby

If you could talk to your baby right now, what would you say to him/her? Would you compose your words as a love-letter, as a poem or lyrics for a song?

You may find this a very emotional exercise and you will pour your heart and soul into your words and, in doing so, I hope you will also find it cathartic.

I have written several pieces through the years – some are love-letters, others are poems. This is an excerpt from one of my favourite poems, written for Meggie in 2013 [iii].

You are always just a whisper away,
This thought brings me comfort
as I think of you each day.
Sometimes I sense you are so very near
and when I whisper your sweet name
I am sure that you hear.
I've often wondered what might have been
to have you here with us.
I close my eyes and try to visualise my girl,
now almost twelve –
and yet you will forever be
that precious tiny baby,
My sweet little Meggie,
my beautiful untouched pearl...
I wonder how tall you'd be,

how long would be your hair,
Of how your eyes would sparkle
as you laugh and smile.
I imagine every detail of your face
and capture that image in my mind's eye
if just for a little while.
You were so much a part
of our hopes and dreams as a family
and while you're gone you are still here,
you have a special place in my heart.

Tell Your Story ...

What will you say to your baby?

Signs From Heaven

A big part of our grief and sadness is a deep longing and yearning to experience our baby with our senses. With that yearning is looking for signs that your baby is near, or perhaps something that is symbolic of him/her.

It might be that you dream of your baby and those dreams feel like you have had a visit from your son/daughter.

Perhaps whenever a butterfly appears, or a rainbow, you think of your baby. It may be a colour that you associate with him/her, or perhaps a scent or a certain sound, a word, a number or an object. Whatever it is, whenever it appears, you automatically think of your baby and you may even see it as a sign that your he/she is communicating with you in a spiritual way.

Many people think of these occurrences as signs from heaven, which bring with them a measure of comfort and peace. These moments may occur in a sequential fashion or they may be few and far between but when they do occur, they are special and the memory of them is cherished. They may even feel mysterious and yet they bring with them the reassurance that your baby is okay, and that he/she is always near, so very near.

I know I have experienced this phenomenon of grief as well. We had one toy in particular that would occasionally play randomly in the still of the night and I would have to go downstairs to stop the noise. Each time I saw this as an opportunity to say hello to Meggie and to thank her for visiting me. I have kept that toy because I'd like to think it is the one thing that all three of my children have played with. Rather than trying to explain it away, I simply choose to marvel in the mystery of it.

I truly believe, as I said in my poem in the previous prompt, that our babies are always just a whisper away.

Tell Your Story ...

Have you ever dreamt about your baby or sensed he/she is near?

Taking That Next Brave Step

For this prompt, I can only speak of my experience as a former IVF patient. Being on stimmed cycles becomes a familiar routine. Each cycle is tracked from Day 1 and the lovely IVF nurses will walk you through your cycle, one step at a time.

For a year I underwent five consecutive cycles. In between that and the next year, we had a short break and then commenced with a further five cycles under a different treatment regime. I have a natural tendency to look for the good in situations, however, even the hope I had held onto so tightly for so long had slowly begun to erode away. In the Preface I mentioned how, with each failed cycle, the disappointment had accumulated to the point where I was forced to consider remaining childless.

Even though this occurred about 25 years ago, I can still clearly remember that failed 10th cycle. We had planned a weekend away up the NSW coast, some four hours away from home. As we arrived at our cabin and were unpacking the car, the bleeding started and it was heavy and painful. I remember finding a large rock to sit on at the water's edge, away from the campsite, and sobbing on the phone to the IVF nurses. I was crushed and, at that time, I didn't think I would ever be able to come back from the feelings of despair and devastation.

That failed 10th cycle was the catalyst for our decision to take a year off from my fertility treatments. It went against my strong maternal drive as I was already in my mid 30s, however, I knew for my physical and mental well-being I needed to take a break. I needed the opportunity to process my experience of infertility and of trying to conceive thus far.

That year-long break also helped mentally prepare me for the next brave step I was about to take: To give it one more try.

Tell Your Story ...

How will you know you are ready to try to conceive again?

Chapter Four:
Self-Care Plan

You Are The Expert Of You

When we experience a loss, it is a circumstance beyond our ability to control. Taking charge of our self-care is one way we can empower ourselves and enable our own coping mechanisms. At a time where everything seems so much harder to manage, doing small simple things can help keep your day-to-day routine at a much more manageable level.

Pregnancy loss will be unlike anything you have experienced before, however, identifying what has been helpful when you have faced losses in the past or other difficult and challenging circumstances, may be a good starting point in figuring out what might help you now. The experience of grief brings our needs to the fore and having a self-care plan is a good way to identify what those needs are and consider how they might be met in a healthy way.

Nobody knows you – and what you need – better than you. One of the most important aspects of self-care is self-awareness. If you are aware of your thoughts, feelings and emotions in the context of your grief and loss, then you will have a better idea of how to keep things at a more manageable level for yourself.

Through the years I have learnt the value of having a written self-care plan. I have found it helpful to look at my needs in the following four categories, which we will look more closely at in the subsequent pages:

1. Mental/Emotional.

2. Physical.

3. Social.

4. Spiritual.

It is understandable that grief and emotional trauma will have an impact on many areas of our daily functioning. As well as the emotional trauma, we experience grief in somatic ways and you may wake feeling exhausted each morning and have very little energy or enthusiasm for the day ahead. As I have said earlier, going through acute grief is, for a time, both exhausting and all-consuming. It slows you down and at times you may need to pace yourself to get through from one hour to the next.

On those days, when everything just seems that little bit harder, having a written self-care plan can be very helpful. Keep it realistic and don't expect too much of yourself. There may just be one or two things that you need to focus your attention on in the here-and-now to help get you through a particularly difficult day.

As you look through the following pages, consider what your specific needs are and how they can be met.

Let's look at each category of self-care and see how they might be relevant to where you're at with your own grief and loss.

Mental and Emotional Well-being

The intensity of grief takes time to work through. Grief in and of itself is hard work. Whilst our emotions and feelings both come from within, we express our emotions outwardly (such as love, joy, sadness and fear). Our feelings, however, are influenced by the thoughts we have regarding our experience. If ever there is a time when our emotions and feelings consume us, then it is with acute grief. As mentioned earlier, it is important to allow ourselves to feel whatever we need to in any given moment – it's okay to be sad, it's also okay to feel happy and there is room for both in your grief.

As mentioned in Chapter Two, love and sadness are the predominant emotions of grief and there are so many thoughts and feelings that we will experience alongside those emotions, and they each have their own place within your grief. Feeling hurt, anxious, misunderstood, guilty, vulnerable, violated, angry, isolated, pressured, and the list goes on.

Let me say loud and clear that there is a reason for whatever you are feeling and, it is my observation, that those more complicated feelings will quite likely stem from unmet needs – and thus, your feelings are valid. We will always default to what feels natural to us. Remember, as complex as our grief is, often our needs are so very simple.

So the question then becomes what is behind a specific feeling and how can you manage it? If, for example, you are feeling anxious, then ask yourself what is causing that anxiety? When you have a better understanding of the underlying cause, then you will have a clearer idea of what you need to do to alleviate your anxiety.

Another important thing to recognise is that some feelings will give way to other feelings. If, for example, you feel misunderstood in your grief then that may frustrate or anger you. If, for example, you feel hurt by something someone has said or done, then you might also feel violated or angry on account of that hurt.

Similarly, if someone shames us for our grief-related feelings – and anger is a good example here because it is often misconstrued as a socially unacceptable behaviour – then we are more likely to subsequently also feel misunderstood and unfairly judged, as well as possibly feeling rejected and unsupported in our grief.

It is my personal experience that with each added layer of unnecessary grief, that becomes one more thing that we have to process and work through. In a very real sense we need to learn to guard our heart so that we can just focus on grieving and healing.

When I was mentally preparing myself for my twins' live birth and stillbirth, I was highly anxious and I recognised that my anxiety stemmed largely from my fear of the unknown. My anxiety would peak at my weekly prenatal appointments, so I would write down in advance what I wanted to ask the doctor about. In understanding why I was feeling so anxious and afraid, I learnt the value of pacing myself and that became a daily practice for me (and it is a practice that I have taken with me through the years).

On the harder days, I would pace myself hour-by-hour and sometimes even breath-by-breath when I needed to. It helped immensely to ground myself in the moment and just focus on one thing that would help me get through that minute, that hour, that day. In that way, I learnt to manage my anxiety and cope as I faced each new unknown of my situation.

Sometimes we underestimate the power of just being still and concentrating on one thing, such as our breathing. Have you tried breathing in slowly through your nose and then slowly, slowly exhaling through your mouth? And all the while just focusing on one thought. Try it now and place your hands on your rib-cage to feel it expand. Do you notice how it feels very different to the shallow breathing we tend to do when we are anxious? It is very different because shallow breathing is more up in the shoulders whereas deep, controlled breathing occurs down in the rib-cage (something I learnt many years ago doing vocal training for singing). I have also noticed when I am anxious I tend to hold my breath!

The techniques for controlled breathing can help us relax and manage pain – both mental and physical – reducing stress and promoting a sense of calm and well-being. This is a good example of one thing you can do just to ground yourself in the moment and it is a technique that you can practice any time, any where.

Our mental health will benefit by doing something as simple as getting outside for some fresh air and sunshine. Sunshine has the added benefit of increasing our levels of the endorphin serotonin (a deficiency of which lends itself to feelings of anxiety and depression).

Addressing your mental and emotional needs may involve talking things through with someone you trust and feel safe with, knowing that they will, with great love and care, listen and convey that they have heard and understood you. It may be eliciting peer support through a pregnancy loss group. It may be eliciting professional support through grief counselling.

It may be reading books and articles about other peoples' stories of grief and loss. I have always found great value in reading about other peoples' experiences, the beauty of which you often see their story in its entirety. Not only are their experiences relatable but they also provide a shared understanding and a hope that grief is survivable.

Perhaps it is working on, or resuming, a creative project that gives you some thinking time or maybe it gives your mind a break from the intensity of your grief. It may be a new creative project that you take on with the sole purpose of memorialising your baby in a meaningful way.

Again, there is no right or wrong way to grieve. It is all about what comes naturally for you, allowing you to work through your emotions and feelings in your own way and time, giving them time to settle.

Tell Your Story ...

What are your needs as you seek to maintain your mental and emotional well-being?

Physical Well-being

As grief is experienced in a somatic way it is, for a time, physically exhausting. At its most acute, we will feel its impact on every aspect of our functioning.

I clearly remember that moment when my mind had registered that Meggie had died and instantaneously I felt the adrenaline kick in. For quite some time, everything seemed to be suspended, especially my appetite and ability to sleep. It felt like my body was protecting me as the reality of her death sunk in.

It is really hard to eat when you have no feelings of hunger. It is hard to sleep when your mind and body are alert. It is hard to think clearly when you're in this state of extreme fatigue. This is also the time when your body needs to be nourished with good food and quality sleep. It is actually the adrenaline that keeps you in this state of heightened alertness.

Listed below are a few thoughts that might be helpful:

- Consider your nutritional needs, together with what foods are easier to prepare and digest... and remember to drink plenty of water.

- Maintain a routine with meal times and bedtime.

- Do something physical, like going for a walk, to help the adrenaline wear off.

- Factor in daily sunshine (even just 10 minutes) for some serotonin and Vitamin D.

- Touch can be a hugely unmet need in grief and skin-on-skin contact is soothing and nurturing for both yourself and your partner.

- And remember, deep controlled breathing is applicable here as well.

Tell Your Story ...

You know what your physical needs are – what do you need to do to take good care of yourself?

Social Needs

If ever there is a time when you need to "gather your village" around you, it is now. You need to know who you can reach out to – the family and friends who will provide you with the emotional safety you need as you work through your grief, your emotions and your memories.

You need those people to be your soft place to fall. You need them to give you the freedom to cry. You need them to keep safe and private the words you entrust to them.

You will know who you can share your grief with. You will know who will be your soft place to fall and who will respect both your privacy and of how vulnerable you are feeling. Those people will respect your grief and you will feel safe in their presence.

There will be days when a coffee date with a trusted friend and change of scenery will be just what you need and you will embrace those opportunities because that friendship is good for your soul. Those friends will share in your tears and your laughter, and just as you would support them in a similar way if the roles were reversed, you know they will make an effort to be there for you when you need some extra support.

However, your grief won't be for everybody. You will know who to set boundaries with when it comes to the more private details of your experience. You may sense that some people are avoiding you or holding back, unable or unwilling to sit with you in your grief. They may wait for you to make the first move, to show when you are ready to face the world again. You may try to make them feel less uncomfortable about your loss, but remember, it isn't your job to make people feel okay about being around you. For now, your job is to grieve and to look after yourself.

Good self-care will recognise that you need to be surrounded by the right people. I reiterate, it is so important to trust your gut instincts with those who gather around you.

Tell Your Story ...

Who will be in the village that gathers around you?

Is there anyone you need to set boundaries with?

Spiritual Connection

Your understanding of spiritual may be in the context of your religion or culture. It may include observing practices and rituals which hold great religious or cultural significance for you and your family – things which affirm your baby's place in your family, within your community and now, as an immortal soul, in the wider universe.

In an ongoing way, the foundation of our spiritual connection is understanding that we can maintain a relationship with our babies, even though they are no longer with us in the physical sense. We already know from our grief that the emotional connection we have with our babies doesn't stop after they have died. That connection is there and it always will be.

In Chapter Three we talked about the signs from heaven and perhaps they play a meaningful role in the spiritual connection you have with your baby.

When I think of the spiritual connection I have with Meggie, I imagine myself sitting on a park bench, watching the sunset. In the physical sense I am alone but I know that Meggie is there too. I imagine her sitting next to me, at the age she would be today. I imagine us talking about the big things and the everyday things. We watch as the soft blue sky gives way to a beautiful golden haze and the sun sinks below the horizon. We simply enjoy this time together. I imagine us both cramming a lifetime of hello's, goodbye's and I love you's into this time together. Unseen in the physical sense, I experience her in a different way.

You will maintain your connection by doing something meaningful which allows peace to enter your heart and help you to smile, albeit through the tears, whenever you think of your baby. Whatever will help that to happen, that's what you will need to do.

Tell Your Story ...

What do you need to do to maintain an ongoing, spiritual connection with your baby?

I will close this book in sharing a poem I wrote in 2017. I want these words to remind you of how amazing you are...

Beautiful, Inside and Out

Look in the mirror, tell me what do you see?
A tummy not as flat as it used to be?
Your eyes have focused on the wrong part
For they haven't yet glimpsed inside your heart.

Look closer, and embrace your inner beauty
Because those who love you, that's what they see.
True, you're not as young as you used to be
(Once so slim and full of energy)
But you tell yourself you're not so pretty.

But here's what I think makes you beautiful –
You love, you care, you think, you feel
And to those who truly know you
You're kind and sincere, your love is real.

My Baby, My Grief, My Love (2025: 2nd Edn)

And this is where you've bared your soul
Where tender lips have kissed, searching for more
Where fingertips have brushed across your skin
And the desire is deeper than ever before.

Now look in the mirror, what do you see?
Right under your heart those little hearts beat
In that sacred inner place as their little bodies grew,
There you nurtured your babies,
So perfect, so sweet.

So now, when you look in the mirror
You'll see there is beauty in the imperfections,
And there are many untold stories
Held within those mirror reflections.

Self-Citations

In this book I have quoted from my previously published book, as cited below:

BRYANT, Julie Ann. From One Twin Mum To Another: An insight into the complexities of multiple birth bereavement. (2022) Melbourne: Busybird Publishing

The self-citations are as follows:

Chapter One: My Baby
[i] p.17 – Chapter One: Naming Your Twins
[ii] p.7 – Chapter One: Julie Ann's Story (Excerpt)

Chapter Three: My Love
[iii] p.5 – Chapter One: Poem

Acknowledgements

John, Tom and Ellis – You have always supported me with your unwavering love. I love you three with my heart and soul. You are my heart and soul.

Meggie – You were here for such a fleeting time but your tiny feet have truly left an indelible mark on my heart. Not a single day has gone by when I haven't stopped to think of you.

David – You are always ready with kind words of reassurance and encouragement. You are my lifelong friend, we have walked many a mile together and I have great love and respect for you.

Deb – My sincere thanks for taking on the challenge of proof-reading the manuscript for this book. Your insights were valuable and your feedback was very much appreciated. You were definitely the right person for this because I know you have a heart for the young grieving couples who will read this book. Deb, we have journeyed together as twin mums for 20 years now and I love you like a sister.

My Baby, My Grief, My Love (2025: 2nd Edn)

Megan – I am grateful for your willingness to write the Foreword for this book, and I thank you for your insightful and kind words. You were one of the first people I connected with through peer support and I am very thankful for the lasting friendship we share.

Julie-Anne – My lovely namesake who, for four years, gave me the time I needed to fully tell my story of grief and trauma. You are the only person who has held that space for me. Listening is one thing, but to convey you have heard and understood is very powerful and empowering. Thank you for being there for me for the many times when I needed a soft place to fall.

My OzMOST Family – Our shared understanding of twin loss goes way beyond empathy and I am ever so grateful that we have embarked on this journey together.

My Busybird Family – Kev and Les, you guys are so awesome and I love being a part of the Busybird family. Your beautiful Blaise's legacy lives on and I think she would be so very proud of you. Don't forget to give Oscar a pat from me and tell him I said he's a good boy.

And last, but certainly not least...

My Baby, My Grief, My Love (2025: 2nd Edn)

To you – the amazing person holding this book in your hands. You have been through a profoundly traumatic experience and I hope you have found my book to be helpful as you navigate your own journey of healing and well-being. I invite you to consider adding a book review to my website – your words could be just what another grieving parent needs to hear. Take good care of you... and thank you.

For more information, visit:
https://julieannbryantauthor.com/

About The Author

Julie Ann Bryant, together with her husband and their two adult children, lives in the Illawarra NSW Australia – a region traditionally known as Dharawal Country, the land of the Wodi Wodi people. She works from home as a medical transcriptionist in radiology.

When her children were young, Julie Ann completed the online Advanced Diploma of Applied Social Science, with her studies focusing on grief and loss. She has a specific interest in disenfranchised grief, especially as it relates to multiple birth bereavement.

In 2022, Julie Ann's first book "From One Twin Mum To Another: An insight into the complexities of multiple birth bereavement" was published. In this book she considers the needs of the grieving parents as they mentally prepare themselves for the impending live birth and stillbirth of their twins and beyond.

Julie Ann's other interests include listening to music, writing poetry and nature photography.

www.ingramcontent.com/pod-product-compliance
Lightning Source LLC
Chambersburg PA
CBHW030329080526
44584CB00012B/772